THE VANCOUVER SUN

the best

pasta

BY CANADA'S BEST-SELLING AUTHORS FROM *THE VANCOUVER SUN* TEST KITCHEN

RUTH PHELAN AND BRENDA THOMPSON

Published by Pacific Newspaper Group,
A division of CanWest MediaWorks Publications Inc.
1-200 Granville Street
Vancouver, B.C.
V6C 3N3

Pacific Newspaper Group President and Publisher:
    Dennis Skulsky

Library and Archives Canada Cataloguing in Publication

Phelan, Ruth, 1960-
    The best pasta / Ruth Phelan and Brenda Thompson.

Includes index.
ISBN 1-897229-04-6

    1. Cookery (Pasta). I. Thompson, Brenda, 1944- II. Title.

TX809.M17P44 2006   641.8'22   C2006-900871-X

Photography by Peter Battistoni

Edited by Shelley Fralic

Nutritional Analysis by Jean Fremont

Printed and bound in Canada by Friesens

First Edition

10 9 8 7 6 5 4 3 2 1

Introduction

There are many reasons why cooks in a hurry turn to pasta: it's quick, easy and nutritious — plus it tastes wonderful and is incredibly satisfying.

In our latest cookbook, full of kitchen-tested, easy-to-follow recipes, we've included a few of the pasta classics (yes, we have recipes utilizing rich cream sauces and delicious cheeses), as well as the more trendy extra-virgin olive oil-based sauces, using newly imported ingredients such as jamon serrano (Spanish ham) and sovrano cheese (similar to parmesan), roasted butternut squash and shallots, and whole-wheat pastas. We also provide substitutions for the less common ingredients.

Pasta is the perfect vehicle for fresh vegetables, adding a wealth of nutrients to our diet. Although the nutritional analysis at the end of each recipe doesn't display the vitamins, minerals and fibre due to a lack of space, be assured that the content of most of the recipes is a rich source of nutrients.

These pasta recipes — a solid sampling of main dishes, soups and salads — are the best to come out of *The Vancouver Sun* Test Kitchen, and many are accompanied by mouth-watering colour photographs courtesy of Sun photographer Peter Battistoni.

We hope that you'll earmark your favourites from these 45 kitchen-tested recipes, compiled for our fourth collection in our *The Best* cookbook series.

Ruth Phelan

Brenda Thompson

Vancouver, B.C.

April 2006

A Cook's Guide to the Recipes

- All recipes use dried pasta unless specified otherwise. We do not specify boiling times for dried pasta because they vary from brand to brand. Please follow the cooking times on the package.

- Cook pasta in large pot of boiling salted water — about 1 tablespoon (15 mL) salt to 4 quarts (4 L) water per ¾ pound (350 g) pasta. If you don't have enough water, the pasta tends to stick together. The water should be at a boil before the pasta is added. Stir the pasta occasionally as it cooks to prevent sticking. Start checking the pasta for doneness a few minutes before the suggested cooking time — you don't want overcooked, mushy pasta.

- Always remove a small amount of the pasta water before draining the pasta — it can be very useful for adding to pasta if the sauce needs a little more moisture.

- Milk is 2 per cent M.F.

- Use medium-size fruit and vegetables unless specified otherwise.

- To toast nuts, place nuts on rimmed baking sheet. Bake at 350 F (180 C) until fragrant and lightly browned — sliced almonds take about 5 minutes and walnuts take 8 to 10 minutes.

- To toast hazelnuts, spread nuts on rimmed baking sheet and bake at 350 F (180 C) for 8 to 10 minutes or until fragrant and lightly browned. Transfer nuts to clean tea towel; roll nuts around, inside towel, to remove as much of the skin as possible. Let cool.

- To toast pine nuts, spread on rimmed baking sheet and bake at 325 F (160 C) for 5 to 8 minutes or until golden.

- Parmesan cheese is freshly grated.

- "Chicken breast" means a single (half) breast, not a double (whole) breast.

- We use Italian (flat-leaf) parsley but you could substitute curly parsley.

- We use extra-virgin olive oil but you could use pure olive oil or vegetable oil.

- "Israeli" couscous, sometimes called pearl or toasted couscous, looks like tiny balls, about the size of peppercorns or pearl tapioca. Look for this pasta in specialty food stores.

Whole-Wheat Spaghetti with Garlic and Olive Oil (recipe on following page)

Mainly Meals

Whole-Wheat Spaghetti with Garlic and Olive Oil

¾   pound (350 g) whole-wheat spaghetti
¼   cup (50 mL) extra-virgin olive oil
2   tablespoons (30 mL) chopped garlic (about 4 large garlic cloves)
½   teaspoon (2 mL) dried crushed hot red pepper
1¼   cups (300 mL) chopped fresh Italian (flat-leaf) parsley
½   cup (125 mL) grated parmesan cheese, divided
     Salt and pepper

Cook spaghetti in large pot of boiling salted water until tender; drain and return to pot. Meanwhile, heat oil in medium-size heavy frypan over low heat. Add garlic and dried red pepper; saute for 8 to 10 minutes or until garlic is fragrant and beginning to turn golden, stirring frequently. (Do not let the garlic turn brown — browned garlic tastes bitter.)

Add garlic mixture, parsley and half the cheese to pasta; toss. Add salt and pepper to taste. Transfer to platter. Sprinkle with remaining cheese.

Tips
• *With so few ingredients, each one has to be a major contributor to the overall flavour of this easy-to-make pasta dish. Choose premium quality ingredients — the best olive oil and parmesan cheese that you can find.*
• *Use freshly grated parmesan cheese, preferably from a block of Parmigiano-Reggiano. Grating takes a few extra minutes, but the difference in flavour and texture is more than worth the time. Avoid the granular parmesan that stands at room temperature on supermarket shelves — it's bland.*
• *To measure whole-wheat spaghetti, grasp a handful of pasta tightly at one end, then measure the diameter — for ¾ pound (350 g) it should measure 1¾ inches (4 cm) across.*
• *Although it's convenient to buy bottled prechopped garlic, we advise using fresh garlic — the flavour is better.*

Makes 4 servings. PER SERVING: 492 cal, 18 g pro, 19 g fat, 67 g carb.

Farfalle with Uncooked Tomato Sauce

2½	cups (625 mL) finely chopped plum tomatoes (about 1 pound/500 g)
1	(398 mL) can red kidney beans, drained and rinsed
½	cup (125 mL) chopped green onions
2	tablespoons (30 mL) chopped fresh basil
2	tablespoons (30 mL) extra-virgin olive oil
2	tablespoons (30 mL) chopped, drained sun-dried tomatoes (packed in oil)
1	garlic clove, minced
3	cups (750 mL) farfalle (medium-size bow-tie pasta)
1½	cups (375 mL) small broccoli florets
1½	cups (375 mL) small cauliflower florets
	Salt and pepper
¼	cup (50 mL) grated parmesan cheese

In large bowl, combine tomatoes, beans, onions, basil, oil, sun-dried tomatoes and garlic; set aside.

Cook farfalle in large pot of boiling salted water until tender, adding broccoli and cauliflower during last 3 minutes of pasta cooking time; drain and return to pot. Add tomato mixture to hot pasta and vegetables; toss. Add salt and pepper to taste. Transfer to platter. Sprinkle with cheese.

Tips
• *For best flavour, choose ripe tomatoes. Tomatoes should be stored at room temperature, not in the refrigerator.*
• *Sun-dried tomatoes (packed in oil) are available in bottles in supermarkets or in small plastic tubs in some delis. The flavour varies, so experiment until you find the ones you like.*

Makes 4 servings. PER SERVING: 487 cal, 20 g pro, 12 g fat, 78 g carb.

Whole-Wheat Spaghetti with Roasted Butternut Squash

4	tablespoons (60 mL) extra-virgin olive oil, divided
2	teaspoons (10 mL) chopped fresh rosemary
	Salt
1	pound (500 g) butternut squash
2	onions
1	tablespoon (15 mL) balsamic vinegar
2	garlic cloves, minced
⅛	teaspoon (0.5 mL) dried crushed hot red pepper
½	cup (125 mL) vegetable stock
¾	pound (350 g) whole-wheat spaghetti
8	cups (2 L) lightly packed fresh baby spinach
½	cup (125 mL) grated asiago cheese

In large bowl, combine 2 tablespoons (30 mL) oil, rosemary and ½ teaspoon (2 mL) salt. Cut butternut squash in half lengthwise; seed, peel and cut into ¾-inch (2 cm) cubes (about 3 cups/750 mL). Peel onions, leaving root end intact; cut each into 8 wedges. Add onions and squash to rosemary mixture; toss. Sprinkle with vinegar; toss. With slotted spoon, remove vegetables from bowl and place, in single layer, on greased large rimmed baking sheet. Bake at 475 (240 C) for 25 to 30 minutes or until tender, turning vegetables halfway through baking time. Add salt to taste. In small saucepan, heat remaining 2 tablespoons (30 mL) oil over medium heat. Add garlic and dried red pepper; cook for 1 minute, stirring constantly. Stir in stock and cook for 2 minutes; set aside.

Ten minutes before end of roasting time, cook spaghetti in pot of boiling salted water until tender, adding spinach during last 30 seconds of pasta cooking time; drain and return to pot. Add garlic mixture; toss. Add roasted vegetables; toss. Transfer to platter. Sprinkle with cheese.

Makes 4 servings. PER SERVING: 600 cal, 21 g pro, 21 g fat, 87 g carb.

Gnocchi with Tomato Sauce

1	(796 mL) can diced tomatoes (undrained)
3	tablespoons (45 mL) extra-virgin olive oil
2	shallots, chopped fine
3	garlic cloves, minced
¼	cup (50 mL) chopped fresh basil
	Salt and pepper
	Pinch dried crushed hot red pepper
1	pound (500 g) fresh potato gnocchi
½	cup (125 mL) grated Italian cheese mix (a blend of mozzarella, provolone, parmesan and fontina)
¼	cup (50 mL) chopped fresh Italian (flat-leaf) parsley

In large heavy saucepan, combine diced tomatoes, oil, shallots, garlic, basil, ½ teaspoon (2 mL) salt and dried red pepper. Bring to a boil over medium-high heat; reduce heat to medium and simmer for 17 minutes, stirring occasionally.

Meanwhile, bring large pot of salted water to a boil. Add gnocchi, a few at a time, and return to a boil over high heat; reduce heat to medium-high and gently boil until tender. Drain gnocchi and add to sauce; gently stir to mix. Add salt and pepper to taste. Transfer to platter. Sprinkle with cheese mix and parsley.

Tips

• *Gnocchi should be extremely light and melt-in-the-mouth. Experiment with brands — some are better than others. We tested with both plain and a herb and ricotta gnocchi that we bought fresh at an Italian deli.*

• *Probably the most expensive of the onion clan, tender shallots are best known for their mild complex flavour. They look like a large garlic bulb and can have 2 or 3 segmented cloves. In our recipes, one shallot refers to the whole bulb not just one clove.*

Makes 4 servings. PER SERVING: 329 cal, 11 g pro, 15 g fat, 43 g carb.

Spaghetti Frittata with Broccoli, Goat Cheese and Sun-Dried Tomatoes

½	pound (250 g) spaghetti, broken in half
2	cups (500 mL) very small broccoli florets
2	tablespoons (30 mL) extra-virgin olive oil
1	small onion, chopped
1	garlic clove, minced
3	tablespoons (45 mL) chopped, drained sun-dried tomatoes (packed in oil)
3	ounces (85 g) unripened soft goat cheese, cut into small pieces
4	large eggs
1	teaspoon (5 mL) salt
¼	teaspoon (1 mL) pepper
1	tablespoon (15 mL) chopped fresh basil
¼	cup (50 mL) grated parmesan cheese

Cook spaghetti in large pot of boiling salted water until tender, adding broccoli during last 2 minutes of pasta cooking time; drain and return to pot.

Meanwhile, heat oil in heavy ovenproof 10-inch (25 cm) frypan over medium heat. Add onion and garlic; saute for 4 minutes or until tender. Stir in sun-dried tomatoes.

Add goat cheese and onion mixture to pasta and broccoli; toss.

Beat together eggs, salt, pepper and basil until blended. Add to pasta mixture; toss. Transfer mixture to frypan and spread evenly with fork. Cook over medium heat for 3 minutes. Sprinkle with parmesan cheese. Bake at 375 F (190 C) for 5 minutes or until eggs are cooked. Cut into wedges.

Makes 4 servings. PER SERVING: 471 cal, 21 g pro, 19 g fat, 54 g carb.

Three Cheese Macaroni

4	cups (1 L) elbow macaroni
1	cup (250 mL) milk
3	large eggs
2	cups (500 mL) grated jalapeno pepper jack cheese
1	cup (250 mL) grated cheddar cheese
¼	cup (50 mL) grated parmesan cheese
2	tablespoons (30 mL) butter
	Salt and pepper
	Chopped fresh Italian (flat-leaf) parsley

Cook macaroni in large heavy pot of boiling salted water until just tender; drain and return to pot.

Meanwhile, beat together milk and eggs until blended. Stir into hot drained pasta (pot shouldn't be on the heat). Add jalapeno pepper jack, cheddar and parmesan cheeses, and butter, stirring until cheese is partially melted. Place over medium-low heat for 5 to 7 minutes or until cheese is melted and sauce is creamy, stirring constantly. Remove from heat, and add salt and pepper to taste. Sprinkle with parsley.

Tips

• *If desired, add diced Black Forest ham, prosciutto (Italian ham) or serrano ham (Spanish ham) to macaroni before serving.*

• *If you prefer a thinner sauce, stir a little warm milk into cheese sauce at the end of cooking time.*

• *Cheese variation: Increase milk to 1½ cups (375 mL). Substitute queso de cabra (hard goat's milk cheese) for the jalapeno pepper jack cheese, part-skim mozzarella for the cheddar cheese and pecorino romano for the parmesan cheese.*

Makes 6 servings. PER SERVING: 590 cal, 29 g pro, 27 g fat, 55 g carb.

Make-Ahead Baked Macaroni and Cheese

Macaroni

3	cups (750 mL) whole-wheat elbow macaroni
1½	cups (375 mL) milk
3	large eggs
4	cups (1 L) grated old cheddar cheese
2	tablespoons (30 mL) butter
¼	teaspoon (1 mL) each salt and pepper

Topping

1	cup (250 mL) soft bread crumbs
2	tablespoons (30 mL) butter, melted
½	cup (125 mL) grated parmesan cheese
¼	teaspoon (1 mL) sweet paprika, optional

Macaroni: Cook macaroni in large heavy pot of boiling salted water until just tender; drain and return to pot.

Meanwhile, beat together milk and eggs until blended. Stir into hot drained pasta (pot shouldn't be on the heat). Add cheese and butter, stirring until cheese is partially melted. Place over medium-low heat for 5 to 7 minutes or until cheese is melted and sauce is creamy, stirring constantly. Remove from heat, and stir in salt and pepper. Transfer to 8-inch (20 cm) square baking dish.

Topping: Put crumbs in small bowl. Sprinkle with butter; toss. Add cheese and paprika; toss.

Sprinkle topping evenly over pasta mixture.

Let stand on rack to cool slightly. Cover tightly with plastic wrap and refrigerate overnight.

To reheat, remove plastic wrap and cover dish loosely with foil. Bake at 350 F (180 C) for 60 minutes. Remove foil and bake for another 15 minutes or until pasta is hot and crumbs are golden.

Tips

• *Make sure the macaroni is boiled until just tender. If the macaroni is overcooked it will soften too much when cooked in the cheese sauce.*

• *Time-saver: Buy grated cheddar cheese. One (400 g) package grated cheddar cheese yields 4 cups (1 L).*

• *One (375 g) package whole-wheat macaroni yields 3 cups (750 mL) uncooked macaroni.*

• *Sliced tomatoes drizzled with olive oil and balsamic vinegar would make an easy accompaniment.*

• *Speedy stove-top variation: Omit crumb topping. Use regular macaroni instead of whole-wheat macaroni and increase to 4 cups (1 L). Reduce milk to 1 cup (250 mL). Don't put pasta and cheese sauce in baking dish – just spoon cooked mixture into serving dishes and sprinkle with parsley.*

Makes 6 servings. PER SERVING: 714 cal, 37 g pro, 39 g fat, 56 g carb.

Whole-Wheat Linguine with Roasted Pumpkin and Shallots

1	(2-pound/1 kg) sugar or pie pumpkin
10	small shallots, peeled
3	tablespoons (45 mL) extra-virgin olive oil
	Salt and pepper
¾	pound (350 g) whole-wheat linguine
2	tablespoons (30 mL) butter
2	garlic cloves, minced
10	large fresh sage leaves
1	cup (250 mL) whipping cream
⅓	cup (75 mL) hazelnuts, toasted and chopped very coarse
⅓	cup (75 mL) chopped fresh Italian (flat-leaf) parsley
½	cup (125 mL) grated pecorino romano cheese

Cut pumpkin lengthwise into quarters; discard seeds and membrane. Peel quarters and cut pumpkin into ¾-inch (2 cm) cubes. Cut any large shallot cloves in half. Put pumpkin cubes and shallots in large bowl. Add oil; toss to coat. Place vegetables, in single layer, on large rimmed baking sheet. Bake at 475 F (240 C) for 20 minutes or until shallots are tender, stirring after 15 minutes. Remove shallots; set aside. Continue baking pumpkin for 5 to 10 minutes or until tender. Sprinkle with ½ teaspoon (2 mL) salt.

Ten minutes before pumpkin comes out of oven, add linguine to large pot of boiling salted water and cook until just tender; drain and return to pot. Meanwhile, heat butter in medium-size heavy frypan over medium-low heat. Add garlic and sage leaves; saute for 1 minute. Remove sage leaves; discard. Add cream to frypan and bring to a boil; boil for 1 minute, stirring frequently. Add pumpkin, shallots, cream mixture, hazelnuts and parsley to pasta; toss. Add salt and pepper to taste. Transfer to platter. Sprinkle with cheese.

Makes 4 servings. PER SERVING: 761 cal, 18 g pro, 44 g fat, 83 g carb.

Ruote with Walnut Pesto

1	cup (250 mL) walnuts, toasted
½	cup (125 mL) grated parmesan cheese
1	teaspoon (5 mL) finely grated lemon zest
4	cups (1 L) tricolour ruote (wagon-wheel pasta)
1	tablespoon (15 mL) extra-virgin olive oil
1	shallot, chopped fine
2	large garlic cloves, minced
¼	teaspoon (1 mL) dried crushed hot red pepper
½	cup (125 mL) cream (10 per cent M.F.)
½	cup (125 mL) whipping cream
	Pinch grated nutmeg
1	tablespoon (15 mL) minced, drained sun-dried tomatoes (packed in oil)
½	cup (125 mL) chopped fresh Italian (flat-leaf) parsley
	Salt and pepper

Process walnuts in food processor until chopped fine; transfer to small bowl, and stir in cheese and zest.

Cook ruote in large pot of boiling salted water until tender; remove ¼ cup (50 mL) pasta water and set aside, then drain pasta and return to pot.

Meanwhile, heat oil in medium-size heavy frypan over medium-low heat. Add shallot, garlic and dried red pepper; saute for 1 minute, stirring constantly. Stir in cream, whipping cream and nutmeg; increase heat to medium-high and bring just to a simmer. Remove from heat; stir in nut mixture and sun-dried tomatoes.

Add cream mixture and parsley to pasta, toss. Add enough of the reserved pasta water to thin sauce to desired consistency. Add salt and pepper to taste.

Makes 4 servings. PER SERVING: 661 cal, 23 g pro, 41 g fat, 54 g carb.

Gemelli with Spinach and Feta Cheese

3   cups (750 mL) gemelli (short pasta twists)
1   pound (500 g) asparagus, trimmed and cut into 1½-inch (4 cm) pieces
2   tablespoons (30 mL) extra-virgin olive oil
3   cups (750 mL) sliced mushrooms
1   onion, chopped
1   large garlic clove, minced
1   small red bell pepper, cut into thin strips
4   cups (1 L) lightly packed fresh baby spinach
½   cup (125 mL) chicken or vegetable stock
2   teaspoons (10 mL) fresh lemon juice
1   (398 mL) can chickpeas, drained and rinsed
½   cup (125 mL) crumbled feta cheese
⅓   cup (75 mL) chopped fresh Italian (flat-leaf) parsley
    Salt and pepper
¼   cup (50 mL) grated parmesan cheese

Cook gemelli in large pot of boiling salted water until tender, adding asparagus pieces during the last 2 to 3 minutes (depending on thickness of stalks) of pasta cooking time; drain and return to pot.

Meanwhile, heat oil in large heavy frypan over medium-high heat. Add mushrooms, onion and garlic; saute for 3 minutes. Add bell pepper; saute for 1 minute. Add spinach; stir until wilted, about 1 minute. Add stock, lemon juice and chickpeas to frypan; cook for 30 seconds or until heated through. Add to pasta and asparagus along with feta cheese and parsley; toss. Add salt and pepper to taste. Transfer to platter. Sprinkle with parmesan cheese.

Tip: *Any short pasta, such as rotini, can be substituted for gemelli.*

Makes 4 servings. PER SERVING: 634 cal, 29 g pro, 19 g fat, 91 g carb.

Farfalle with Asparagus and Snow Peas

4	cups (1 L) farfalle (medium-size bow-tie pasta)
1	pound (500 g) asparagus, trimmed and cut into 1½-inch (4 cm) pieces
¼	pound (125 g) snow peas, trimmed (cut any large peas in half)
2	tablespoons (30 mL) extra-virgin olive oil, divided
1	small onion, cut in half lengthwise and sliced thin
3	garlic cloves, minced
6	plum tomatoes, cut into small pieces
2	tablespoons (30 mL) chopped, drained sun-dried tomatoes (packed in oil)
1	tablespoon (15 mL) fresh lemon juice
¼	cup (50 mL) shredded fresh basil
¼	cup (50 mL) grated parmesan cheese
	Salt and pepper
	Grated parmesan cheese, optional

Cook farfalle in large pot of boiling salted water until tender, adding asparagus pieces during the last 2 to 3 minutes (depending on thickness of stalks) of pasta cooking time and snow peas for the last 2 minutes of cooking time. Drain and return to pot. Add 1 tablespoon (15 mL) oil; toss.

Meanwhile, heat remaining 1 tablespoon (15 mL) oil in large heavy frypan over medium-high heat. Add onion and garlic; saute for 2 minutes or until onion is tender. Add plum tomatoes; cook for 2 minutes or until just heated through. Stir in sun-dried tomatoes, lemon juice and basil. Add to pasta mixture; toss. Add ¼ cup (50 mL) cheese; toss. Add salt and pepper to taste; toss. Transfer to platter. If desired, sprinkle with additional cheese.

Makes 4 servings. PER SERVING: 368 cal, 15 g pro, 11 g fat, 56 g carb.

Quick and Easy Baked Ravioli

1¾	cups (425 mL) grated part-skim mozzarella cheese
½	cup (125 mL) grated parmesan cheese
2	tablespoons (30 mL) extra-virgin olive oil
1	onion, chopped
2	large garlic cloves, minced
2	cups (500 mL) sliced mushrooms
1	(540 mL) can tomatoes (undrained), chopped coarse
1	(700 mL) jar tomato and basil pasta sauce
4	cups (1 L) lightly packed fresh baby spinach, chopped coarse
2	(350 g) packages fresh ravioli stuffed with spinach and cheese
	Salt and pepper
¼	cup (50 mL) chopped fresh Italian (flat-leaf) parsley

In small bowl, combine mozzarella and parmesan cheeses.

In 12-inch (30 cm) heavy frypan, heat oil over medium-high heat. Add onion, garlic and mushrooms; saute for 5 minutes or until onion and mushrooms are tender. Add tomatoes and pasta sauce; bring to a boil, reduce heat and simmer for 5 minutes. Stir in spinach; set aside.

Cook ravioli in large pot of boiling salted water for 1 minute (do not overcook); drain and return to pot. Add tomato mixture; toss. Transfer to 13x9-inch (33x23 cm) baking dish. Sprinkle with cheese mixture.

Bake at 400 F (200 C) for 23 to 25 minutes or until cheese is lightly browned. Let stand for 5 minutes before serving. Sprinkle with salt and pepper to taste. Sprinkle with parsley.

Tip: *To make sauce ahead, cook tomato sauce (do not add spinach). Let cool slightly, cover and refrigerate overnight. When ready to use, bring sauce to a simmer and add spinach. Cook ravioli and continue with recipe.*

Makes 8 servings. PER SERVING: 472 cal, 21 g pro, 23 g fat, 46 g carb.

Risotto-Style Orzo with Basil

2	tablespoons (30 mL) extra-virgin olive oil
1	large shallot, chopped fine
1	garlic clove, minced
1½	cups (375 mL) orzo (rice-shaped pasta)
3	cups (750 mL) chicken stock
⅔	cup (150 mL) grated sovrano or parmesan cheese
¼	cup (50 mL) shredded fresh basil
	Salt and pepper

In large heavy frypan, heat oil over medium heat. Add shallot and garlic; saute for 1 minute, stirring constantly. Add orzo; saute for 2 minutes, stirring constantly. Add stock; increase heat to medium-high and bring to a boil. Reduce heat, cover and simmer until orzo is tender and liquid is absorbed, about 20 to 25 minutes.

Remove from heat; stir in cheese and basil. Add salt and pepper to taste.

Tips

• *Often the fresh basil available in supermarkets during the winter months can have a strong, almost bitter flavour. Taste the basil and reduce the amount used if necessary.*

• *This risotto-style creamy pasta dish makes a comforting side for roasted chicken or grilled seafood.*

Makes 4 servings. PER SERVING: 288 cal, 12 g pro, 12 g fat, 32 g carb.

Scoobi Doo with Chicken and Edamame

2	small boneless skinless chicken breasts, cut into bite-size pieces
	Salt and pepper
2	tablespoons (30 mL) extra-virgin olive oil, divided
1	small onion, chopped
1	large garlic clove, minced
4	cups (1 L) scoobi doo (hollow, spiral-shaped pasta)
2	cups (500 mL) sliced brown mushrooms
¾	cup (175 mL) chicken stock
3	tablespoons (45 mL) chopped, drained sun-dried tomatoes (packed in oil)
1	teaspoon (5 mL) finely chopped fresh rosemary
⅛	teaspoon (0.5 mL) dried crushed hot red pepper
2	cups (500 mL) frozen shelled edamame (green soybeans)
½	pound (250 g) asparagus, trimmed and cut into 1½-inch (4 cm) pieces
¼	pound (125 g) snow peas, trimmed (2 cups/500 mL)
⅓	cup (75 mL) grated asiago cheese

Lightly sprinkle chicken with salt and pepper. In large heavy frypan, heat 1 tablespoon (15 mL) oil over medium-high heat. Add chicken, onion and garlic; saute for 6 minutes or until onion is tender and chicken is no longer pink inside. Transfer chicken mixture to bowl; cover and set aside.

Meanwhile, cook pasta in large pot of boiling salted water until tender; drain and return to pot. Add chicken mixture; toss. Cover and set aside.

Add remaining 1 tablespoon (15 mL) oil to frypan and place over medium heat. Add mushrooms; saute for about 3 minutes or until mushrooms are tender. Add stock, sun-dried tomatoes, rosemary and dried red pepper; bring to a boil and cook for 1 minute, stirring constantly. Add to pasta mixture; toss. Cover and set aside.

In large saucepan of boiling water, add edamame and return to the boil. Add asparagus; cook for 2 minutes. Add snow peas; cook for 1 minute or until vegetables are tender-crisp. Drain and add to pasta mixture; toss. Add salt and pepper to taste. Transfer to platter. Sprinkle with cheese.

Tips

• For ease of preparation, be sure to prepare and measure all of the ingredients before commencing to cook. Bring two pots of water to the boil, and leave at the ready.

• You may come across some packages of spiral-shaped pasta labelled tortiglioni — it is very similar in shape to scoobi doo. Tortiglioni, or any other short spiral-shaped pasta such as fusilli or rotini, can be substituted for scoobi doo pasta.

Makes 5 servings. PER SERVING: 527 cal, 34 g pro, 17 g fat, 63 g carb.

Rotini with Asparagus and Light Alfredo Sauce

4	cups (1 L) rotini
1	pound (500 g) asparagus, trimmed and cut into 1½-inch (4 cm) pieces
1	tablespoon (15 mL) extra-virgin olive oil
¾	pound (350 g) boneless skinless chicken breasts, cut into thin strips
	Salt and pepper
1	large shallot, chopped fine
1	small garlic clove, minced
	Pinch dried crushed hot red pepper
1	(300 mL) pouch refrigerated light alfredo pasta sauce
¼	cup (50 mL) milk
¼	cup (50 mL) grated parmesan cheese
2	tablespoons (30 mL) chopped green onion

In large pot of boiling salted water cook rotini until tender, adding asparagus pieces during last 2 to 3 minutes (depending on thickness of stalks) of pasta cooking time; drain and return to pot.

Meanwhile, heat oil in large nonstick frypan over medium heat. Lightly sprinkle chicken with salt and pepper; add to frypan and cook for 3 minutes or until no longer pink inside. With slotted spoon, transfer chicken to plate; keep warm.

Add shallot, garlic and dried red pepper to frypan; reduce heat to medium-low and saute for 1 minute. Add pasta sauce and milk; simmer for 1 minute. Return chicken to frypan and heat through, about 1 minute. Add chicken mixture to pasta and asparagus; toss. Add salt and pepper to taste. Transfer to platter. Sprinkle with cheese and onion.

Makes 4 servings. PER SERVING: 537 cal, 40 g pro, 13 g fat, 65 g carb.

Tortelloni with Mushrooms and Bell Pepper

1   (350 g) package fresh turkey tortelloni
2   cups (500 mL) bottled tomato-based pasta sauce
1   tomato, chopped coarse
2   tablespoons (30 mL) extra-virgin olive oil
1   small onion, chopped
2   cups (500 mL) sliced mushrooms
1   small yellow bell pepper, sliced
1   small zucchini, sliced
    Salt and pepper
2   tablespoons (30 mL) grated parmesan cheese

Cook tortelloni in large pot of boiling salted water according to package directions; drain and return to pot.

Meanwhile, put pasta sauce and tomato in medium-size heavy saucepan. Cook over medium heat until hot, stirring occasionally; keep warm.

While sauce is cooking, heat oil in large heavy frypan over medium-high heat. Add onion; saute for 2 minutes. Add mushrooms; saute for 2 minutes. Add bell pepper; saute for 1 minute. Add zucchini; saute for 2 minutes or until vegetables are tender. Add salt and pepper to taste. Add vegetables to tortelloni; toss. Transfer to platter and top with pasta sauce. Sprinkle with cheese.

Tips

• *Tortelloni look like tortellini that have been spending time at the gym: they're bigger, pumped up. Of course, if you can't find tortelloni, simply use any small stuffed fresh pasta.*
• *For a vegetarian version, use a cheese or vegetable-filled tortelloni.*

Makes 4 servings. PER SERVING: 401 cal, 17 g pro, 14 g fat, 56 g carb.

Make-Ahead Mushroom and Sausage Lasagne

Tomato filling

1	tablespoon (15 mL) extra-virgin olive oil
½	pound (250 g) hot or mild Italian sausages, casings removed
1	onion, chopped
2	garlic cloves, minced
2	pounds (1 kg) mushrooms, sliced thin (12 cups/3 L)
1	(700 mL) jar tomato and basil pasta sauce
1	teaspoon (5 mL) dried oregano leaves, crumbled
	Dash hot pepper sauce, optional
	Salt and pepper

Cheese filling

1	(500 g) container ricotta cheese (2 cups/500 mL)
1	cup (250 mL) grated provolone cheese
¾	cup (175 mL) grated parmesan cheese
2	large eggs
½	cup (125 mL) chopped fresh Italian (flat-leaf) parsley
½	teaspoon (2 mL) each salt and pepper

Other ingredients

9	lasagne noodles
2	cups (500 mL) grated provolone cheese
¼	cup (50 mL) grated parmesan cheese

Tomato filling: In large pot, heat oil over medium-high heat. Add sausage, onion and garlic; saute for 5 minutes or until sausage is well browned, stirring frequently to break up meat. Add mushrooms; saute for 18 minutes or until all the liquid has been released and has evaporated. Stir in pasta sauce, oregano, hot pepper sauce, and salt and pepper to taste; set aside.

Cheese filling: In large bowl, whisk together ricotta, provolone and parmesan cheeses, eggs, parsley, salt and pepper.

Cook lasagne noodles in large pot of boiling salted water until just tender; drain and rinse with cold water. Immediately place noodles flat on tea towel to remove excess moisture.

Assembly: Spread ⅓ of tomato filling (about 2 cups/500 mL) over bottom of 13x9-inch (33x23 cm) baking dish. Place 3 noodles over top. Spread half of the cheese filling (about 1½ cups/375 mL) over noodles. Top with ⅓ of the tomato filling. Top with 3 lasagne noodles. Spread remaining cheese filling over noodles. Top with remaining lasagne noodles and tomato filling, then 2 cups (500 mL) provolone cheese. Sprinkle with ¼ cup (50 mL) parmesan cheese.

Lightly grease one side of a large piece of foil. Cover lasagne with foil, greased side down. Bake at 375 F (190 C) for 20 minutes; remove foil and continue baking for 20 to 25 minutes or until bubbling and heated through. Remove from oven; let stand for 10 minutes before serving.

Tips

• *To make a day ahead: Cover unbaked lasagne with a greased piece of foil, greased side down, and refrigerate overnight. Before baking, let stand, covered, at room temperature for 20 minutes. Add an additional 30 minutes to first baking time (when covered with foil).*

• *To freeze: Cover unbaked lasagne with a greased piece of foil, greased side down; overwrap tightly with heavy-duty foil and freeze for up to 2 weeks. Let thaw in refrigerator, about 48 hours. Before baking, remove from refrigerator and remove overwrap of foil; let stand, covered, at room temperature for 20 minutes. Add an additional 30 minutes to first baking time (when covered with foil).*

• *Use regular lasagne noodles that have to be cooked before layering — the oven-ready (no-boil) noodles are not suitable for this make-ahead recipe (they'd absorb too much liquid, resulting in dried-out lasagne).*

Makes 8 servings. PER SERVING: 684 cal, 37 g pro, 38 g fat, 50 g carb.

Rotini with Hot Italian Sausages

4	cups (1 L) rotini
1	tablespoon (15 mL) extra-virgin olive oil
½	pound (250 g) hot Italian sausages, casings removed
1	small onion, chopped
1	garlic clove, minced
1	small zucchini, cut into ¼-inch (5 mm) thick slices
1	cup (250 mL) sliced mushrooms
1	(700 mL) jar tomato and basil pasta sauce
	Pinch granulated sugar
	Salt and pepper
¼	cup (50 mL) grated parmesan cheese

Cook rotini in large pot of boiling salted water until tender; drain and return to pot.

Meanwhile, heat oil in large heavy frypan over medium heat. Add sausage; cook for 5 minutes or until cooked, stirring and breaking up any lumps. With slotted spoon, remove sausage; set aside.

Add onion, garlic and zucchini to frypan; saute for 3 minutes. Add mushrooms; saute for 3 minutes. Return sausage to frypan; stir in pasta sauce and sugar. Cook for 3 minutes or until heated through. Add salt and pepper to taste.

Add sausage mixture to pasta; toss. Transfer to platter. Sprinkle with cheese.

Tip: *For a fresher tasting sauce, chop a ripe tomato and add it to the sauce with the pasta sauce.*

Makes 4 servings. PER SERVING: 866 cal, 30 g pro, 31 g fat, 118 g carb.

Whole-Wheat Rotini with Lentils and Kielbasa

3	tablespoons (45 mL) extra-virgin olive oil, divided
2	teaspoons (10 mL) red wine vinegar
1	teaspoon (5 mL) dijon mustard
	Salt and pepper
¼	pound (125 g) kielbasa sausage, sliced thin
2	carrots, diced fine
2	celery stalks, diced fine
1	onion, chopped fine
2	garlic cloves, minced
1½	cups (375 mL) chicken stock, divided
1	(540 mL) can lentils, drained and rinsed
1	tablespoon (15 mL) chopped fresh rosemary
3	cups (750 mL) whole-wheat rotini
¼	cup (50 mL) chopped fresh Italian (flat-leaf) parsley

In small bowl, whisk together 2 tablespoons (30 mL) oil, vinegar, mustard, and ¼ teaspoon (5 mL) each salt and pepper; set aside.

In large heavy frypan, heat remaining 1 tablespoon (15 mL) oil over medium heat. Add sausage; saute for about 2 minutes or until lightly browned. With slotted spoon, remove sausage; set aside.

Add carrots, celery, onion and garlic to frypan; saute for about 5 minutes or until onion is tender-crisp, stirring frequently. Add 1¼ cups (300 mL) stock; simmer for 8 minutes or until most of the liquid is absorbed and vegetables are tender. Stir in sausage, lentils and rosemary; cook for 1 minute. Stir in remaining ¼ cup (50 mL) stock.

Meanwhile, cook rotini in large pot of boiling salted water until tender; drain and return to pot. Add sausage, vegetable mixture and parsley; toss. Drizzle with vinegar mixture; toss. Add salt and pepper to taste.

Makes 4 servings. PER SERVING: 602 cal, 25 g pro, 21 g fat, 85 g carb.

Tortiglioni with Tuscan Kale and Shiitake Mushrooms

2½   tablespoons (37 mL) extra-virgin olive oil, divided
2   ounces (60 g) thinly sliced pancetta (Italian bacon), chopped
1   onion, chopped
2   large garlic cloves, minced
    Pinch dried crushed hot red pepper
¼   pound (125 g) shiitake mushrooms, stemmed and sliced thin
1   red bell pepper, cut into small pieces
4   cups (1 L) tortiglioni (large spiral-edged pasta tubes)
1   pound (500 g) Tuscan (lacinato) or regular green kale, stemmed and chopped coarse (about 12 cups/3 L)
¾   cup (175 mL) chicken stock
1   teaspoon (5 mL) fresh lemon juice
    Salt and pepper
¼   cup (50 mL) pine nuts, toasted
¼   cup (50 mL) grated parmesan cheese

In large heavy pot, heat 1 tablespoon (15 mL) oil over medium heat. Add pancetta; saute until crisp. With slotted spoon, transfer to plate. Add onion, garlic and dried red pepper to pot; saute 2 minutes. Add mushrooms; saute 3 minutes. Add bell pepper; saute 1 minute or until vegetables are tender. With slotted spoon, transfer to bowl.

Cook tortiglioni in large pot of boiling salted water until tender; drain and return to pot.

Meanwhile, heat remaining 1½ tablespoons (22 mL) oil in same pot that pancetta was cooked in. Add half the kale; saute 30 seconds. Add remaining kale; saute 1 minute. Add stock; cover, reduce heat and simmer 3 minutes or until kale is tender. Return mushroom mixture and pancetta to pot; cook 1 minute or until heated through. Add to pasta, with lemon juice, and salt and pepper to taste; toss. Transfer to platter. Sprinkle with pine nuts and cheese.

Makes 4 servings. PER SERVING: 604 cal, 23 g pro, 20 g fat, 88 g carb.

Rigatoni with Vodka Sauce

2	tablespoons (30 mL) extra-virgin olive oil
1	ounce (30 g) thinly sliced prosciutto, chopped coarse
1	onion, chopped
2	large garlic cloves, minced
1	(540 mL) can whole tomatoes (undrained), chopped
1	(398 mL) can stewed tomatoes (undrained), chopped
½	cup (125 mL) vodka
¼	cup (50 mL) whipping cream
2	tablespoons (30 mL) chopped fresh basil
	Salt and pepper
4	cups (1 L) rigatoni or penne
¼	cup (50 mL) chopped fresh Italian (flat-leaf) parsley
⅓	cup (75 mL) grated parmesan cheese

In 10-inch (25 cm) heavy frypan, heat oil over medium-low heat. Add prosciutto; saute for 3 minutes or until crisp. With slotted spoon, remove prosciutto; set aside.

Add onion and garlic to frypan; saute for 3 minutes or until onion is tender. Add whole tomatoes, stewed tomatoes and vodka; increase heat to medium and bring to a boil. Reduce heat to medium-low and cook at a slow boil for 25 minutes or until slightly thickened, stirring occasionally. *(Make ahead: Let sauce cool slightly, then transfer to heatproof bowl, cover and refrigerate overnight. When ready to use, pour into frypan and bring to a simmer over medium heat.)*

Remove frypan from heat and stir in cream and basil; return to heat and cook over low heat for 1 minute or just until heated through (do not boil). Remove from heat. Add salt and pepper to taste.

Meanwhile, cook rigatoni in large pot of boiling salted water until tender; drain and return to pot. Add tomato mixture; toss. Sprinkle with prosciutto, parsley and cheese.

Makes 4 servings. PER SERVING: 516 cal, 15 g pro, 14 g fat, 67 g carb.

Baby Bell Peppers Stuffed with Couscous

2	tablespoons (30 mL) pine nuts
8	Sweet Baby (mini) bell peppers
⅓	cup (75 mL) chicken stock
2	teaspoons (10 mL) grated lemon zest
1	tablespoon (15 mL) fresh lemon juice
3	tablespoons (45 mL) regular (instant) couscous
2	tablespoons (30 mL) currants
1	tablespoon (15 mL) extra-virgin olive oil
¼	cup (50 mL) finely chopped onion
1	large garlic clove, minced
1	ounce (30 g) thinly sliced prosciutto, chopped
2	tablespoons (30 mL) chopped fresh Italian (flat-leaf) parsley
1	tablespoon (15 mL) chopped pitted kalamata olives
2	teaspoons (10 mL) drained capers, chopped
¼	teaspoon (1 mL) salt
⅛	teaspoon (0.5 mL) pepper

Put pine nuts in heavy frypan over medium heat. Toast nuts for 3 to 5 minutes or until golden, stirring frequently. Remove nuts to bowl; set aside.

Using a small sharp knife, cut a ½-inch (1 cm) wedge of bell pepper lengthwise out of one side of each bell pepper; finely dice wedges and set aside. Using knife and handle of small spoon, carefully remove seeds from each pepper.

Put stock, and lemon zest and juice in microwaveable 1-cup (250 ml) measure. Microwave on High until stock comes to a boil. Stir in couscous, then currants; cover measuring cup tightly with plastic wrap and let stand for 5 minutes. Fluff with fork and cover.

Meanwhile, heat oil in same frypan over medium heat. Add onion, garlic, prosciutto and reserved diced bell pepper; saute for 3 to 5 minutes or until vegetables are tender-crisp. Remove from heat; add pine nuts, parsley, olives and capers.

Fluff couscous again and add to sauteed vegetable-prosciutto mixture in frypan; stir to mix. Add salt and pepper. Using a teaspoon, fill each bell pepper with couscous mixture and place in lightly oiled baking dish leaving space in between peppers. *(Make ahead: Stuffed peppers can be covered tightly and refrigerated for up to 24 hours. Remove from refrigerator and let stand at room temperature for 1 hour before baking.)* Bake at 400 F (200 C) for 18 to 20 minutes or until tender but not collapsing.

Tips
• Before cutting wedges from bell peppers, lay peppers lengthwise on flat work surface and rotate to find out where they will lie flat naturally (this prevents them from turning over after they're stuffed).
• After baking, these peppers hold their shape and colour well, making them an easy, special-occasion accompaniment to grilled fish, chicken or roast lamb.

Makes 4 servings. PER SERVING: 136 cal, 5 g pro, 8 g fat, 15 g carb.

Spinach Fettuccine with Four Cheeses

¾   pound (350 g) spinach fettuccine
1   tablespoon (15 mL) extra-virgin olive oil
2   ounces (60 g) thinly sliced prosciutto, chopped
2   large shallots, chopped fine
1   cup (250 mL) cream (10 per cent M.F.), divided
½   cup (125 mL) grated emmental cheese
½   cup (125 mL) grated pecorino romano cheese
¼   cup (50 mL) Danish blue cheese (about 2 ounces/60 g)
      Salt and pepper
1   tablespoon (15 mL) dry white wine
¼   cup (50 mL) grated parmesan cheese
¼   cup (50 mL) chopped fresh basil
¼   cup (50 mL) coarsely chopped fresh Italian (flat-leaf) parsley

Cook fettuccine in large pot of boiling salted water until tender; remove ½ cup (125 mL) pasta water and set aside, then drain pasta and return to pot. Meanwhile, heat oil in large heavy frypan over medium-low heat. Add prosciutto; saute for about 3 minutes or until crisp. Add shallots; saute for 1 minute. With slotted spoon, remove prosciutto and shallots; set aside. Add ¾ cup (175 mL) cream to frypan and heat for 2 minutes (do not boil), whisking constantly. Whisk in emmental, pecorino romano and blue cheeses, and ¼ teaspoon (1 mL) each salt and pepper. Cook for 1 to 2 minutes or until cheese has melted and sauce is creamy, whisking constantly. Add wine and whisk until blended.

Add cheese mixture to pasta; toss. Add remaining ¼ cup (50 mL) cream, parmesan cheese, basil and prosciutto-shallot mixture; toss. Add salt and pepper to taste. Add enough of the reserved pasta water to thin sauce to desired consistency. Transfer to platter. Sprinkle with parsley.

Makes 6 servings. PER SERVING: 427 cal, 20 g pro, 17 g fat, 47 g carb.

Farfalle with Prosciutto and Sovrano Cheese

1	cup (250 mL) frozen small peas
4	cups (1 L) farfalle (medium-size bow-tie pasta)
1	tablespoon (15 mL) butter
1	tablespoon (15 mL) extra-virgin olive oil
1	onion, chopped
1	leek (white and pale green part only), sliced thin
2	large garlic cloves, minced
2	ounces (30 g) thinly sliced prosciutto, chopped coarse
¾	cup (175 mL) cream (10 per cent M.F.), divided
½	cup (125 mL) whipping cream
1	cup (250 mL) grated sovrano or parmesan cheese, divided
⅓	cup (75 mL) chopped fresh Italian (flat-leaf) parsley
	Salt and pepper

Place frozen peas in strainer and rinse with cold water until partially thawed; set aside.

Cook farfalle in large pot of boiling salted water until tender, adding peas during last 2 minutes of pasta cooking time; drain and return to pot.

Meanwhile, heat butter and oil in large heavy frypan over medium heat. Add onion, leek, garlic and prosciutto; saute 10 minutes or until onion is tender. Add ½ cup (125 mL) cream and whipping cream. Increase heat to medium-high; bring just to a simmer. Add to pasta; toss.

Add remaining ¼ cup (50 mL) cream, ⅔ cup (150 mL) cheese and parsley to pasta; toss. Add salt and pepper to taste. Sprinkle with remaining ⅓ cup (75 mL) cheese.

Tip: Sovrano is made from a combination of buffalo and cow's milk. It is similar in appearance and texture to a good quality parmesan cheese but it has a slightly creamier texture and milder flavour.

Makes 4 servings. PER SERVING: 580 cal, 25 g pro, 32 g fat, 50 g carb.

Beef Stroganoff with Spanish Smoked Sweet Paprika

Noodles

6	cups (1.5 L) pappardelle (wide pasta ribbons)
1	tablespoon (15 mL) butter
¼	cup (50 mL) chopped fresh chives
	Salt and pepper

Beef sauce

4	teaspoons (20 mL) all-purpose flour
½	teaspoon (2 mL) Spanish smoked sweet paprika
	Salt and pepper
¾	pound (350 g) beef sirloin steak, cut into thin strips
2	tablespoons (30 mL) extra-virgin olive oil, divided
1	onion, chopped
3	cups (750 mL) sliced brown mushrooms
2	large garlic cloves, minced
1	cup (250 mL) beef stock
1	tablespoon (15 mL) ketchup
1	cup (250 mL) thick plain yogurt (10 per cent M.F.)
⅓	cup (75 mL) chopped fresh Italian (flat-leaf) parsley

Noodles: Cook pappardelle in large pot of boiling salted water until tender; drain and return to pot. Add butter, chives, and salt and pepper to taste; toss.

Meanwhile, make beef sauce: In small bowl, combine flour, paprika, ½ teaspoon (2 mL) salt and ¼ teaspoon (1 mL) pepper; set aside. Lightly sprinkle steak with salt.

In large heavy frypan, heat 1 tablespoon (15 mL) oil over medium-high heat. Add steak and saute for 3 to 5 minutes or until no longer pink. Remove steak; set aside. Reduce heat to medium.

Add remaining 1 tablespoon (15 mL) oil to frypan. Add onion, mushrooms and garlic; saute for 5 to 6 minutes or until vegetables are tender.

Increase heat to high, return steak to frypan and sprinkle with flour mixture; cook for 1 minute, stirring constantly. Stir in stock and ketchup; cook for 2 minutes, stirring constantly. Remove pan from heat; stir in yogurt and parsley. Add salt and pepper to taste. Transfer noodles to platter. Spoon sauce over top.

Tips

• *Finding the thick plain yogurt may take a little searching, but it's well worth the hunt. (We used Liberty Mediterranee brand of yogurt.) Refrain from substituting a low-fat plain yogurt, as the resulting dish will taste slightly sour and the texture of the sauce will be thin and grainy. Light sour cream can be substituted but it doesn't have quite the same creamy texture and fresh flavour as the thick yogurt.*

• *You can substitute regular paprika for the Spanish smoked sweet paprika but the dish won't have the delightfully distinct smoky flavour.*

• *Broad egg noodles could easily stand in for pappardelle.*

Makes 4 servings. PER SERVING: 545 cal, 32 g pro, 22 g fat, 55 g carb.

One-Pot Beef Rotini

1	portion frozen Basic Beef Mixture, thawed (see recipe, page 52)
1	(796 mL) can diced tomatoes
1	(213 mL) can tomato sauce
2	cups (500 mL) water
½	teaspoon (2 mL) dried basil leaves
½	teaspoon (2 mL) dried oregano leaves
3	cups (750 mL) rotini
	Salt and pepper
¼	cup (50 mL) grated parmesan cheese

In large saucepan, combine meat mixture, tomatoes, tomato sauce, water, basil and oregano; cover and bring to a boil over high heat. Add rotini and reduce heat to medium-low; cover and simmer for about 13 minutes or until pasta is tender, stirring occasionally. Add salt and pepper to taste. Serve sprinkled with cheese.

Tip: *Commercial pasta sauce variation: Omit canned diced tomatoes, tomato sauce, basil and oregano. Add 1 (700 mL) jar tomato and basil pasta sauce and increase water to 3 cups (750 mL).*
"Just like Chef Boyardee," said one of our testers, who sampled this dish made with store-bought pasta sauce. (We think it was a compliment.) Both variations — made with canned tomatoes or pasta sauce — were gobbled up, so we know either will be a midweek hit.

Makes 4 servings. PER SERVING: 554 cal, 31 g pro, 13 g fat, 80 g carb.

Basic Beef Mixture

2¼ pounds (1 kg) lean ground beef
3   onions, chopped
6   large garlic cloves, chopped
4½ cups (1.125 L) sliced mushrooms (about ¾ pound/350 g)

In large heavy frypan, saute beef over medium-high heat for 10 minutes or until no longer pink, breaking up with a spoon and stirring frequently. With slotted spoon, transfer beef to large bowl; set aside.

Discard all but 1 tablespoon (15 mL) liquid from frypan. Add onions, garlic and mushrooms; saute for 8 minutes or until mushrooms and onions are tender, and excess liquid has evaporated, stirring occasionally. Add to beef in bowl and stir to mix; let cool.

Divide mixture into 3 equal portions (about 2½ cups/625 mL each). Place each portion in medium-size freezer bag; pat to remove excess air, then seal and press bag to flatten. Store in freezer for up to 1 month.

To thaw: Can be thawed overnight in refrigerator. To thaw quickly, remove beef from bag and place in medium bowl; cover with vented plastic wrap and microwave on High for 2½ minutes or until thawed, stirring once.

Tips
• *With portions of this beef mixture stored in the freezer, making One-Pot Beef Rotini (see page 51) is a snap.*
• *You can saute this large amount of ground beef in a heavy frypan without using oil — there will be enough liquid released from the beef to prevent it from sticking to the pan.*

Makes 3 portions. PER PORTION: 559 cal, 64 g pro, 28 g fat, 9 g carb.

Cheesy Pasta Shells with Ham

3	cups (750 mL) medium-size pasta shells
2	cups (500 mL) grated part-skim mozzarella cheese, divided
1	cup (250 mL) plain low-fat yogurt
1	cup (250 mL) low-fat cottage cheese
1½	cups (375 mL) diced ham (about 6 ounces/170 g)
1	large egg, lightly beaten
3	green onions, chopped
1	teaspoon (5 mL) dijon mustard
¼	teaspoon (1 mL) each salt and pepper
¼	cup (50 mL) grated parmesan cheese
	Chopped fresh Italian (flat-leaf) parsley

Cook shells in large heavy pot of boiling salted water until tender; drain and return to pot.

Meanwhile, in large bowl, combine 1½ cups (375 mL) mozzarella cheese, yogurt, cottage cheese, ham, egg, onions, mustard, salt and pepper; add to pasta. Cook over medium heat for 2 to 3 minutes or until heated through and cheese melts, stirring constantly.

Transfer mixture to greased 8-inch (20 cm) square broiler-proof baking dish. Sprinkle with remaining mozzarella cheese and parmesan cheese. Place under broiler for 2 to 4 minutes or until golden. Sprinkle with parsley.

Tip: *You will require a broiler-proof baking dish for this recipe.*

Makes 4 servings. PER SERVING: 827 cal, 69 g pro, 30 g fat, 67 g carb.

Spaghetti with Clams and Gremolata

⅓   cup (75 mL) extra-virgin olive oil, divided
2   ounces (60 g) thinly sliced pancetta (Italian bacon), chopped
¼   cup (50 mL) chopped onion
4   garlic cloves, minced
¼   teaspoon (1 mL) dried crushed hot red pepper
2   pounds (1 kg) manila clams, scrubbed
⅓   cup (75 mL) dry white wine
½   cup (125 mL) coarsely chopped Italian (flat-leaf) parsley, divided
     Salt and pepper
1   tablespoon (15 mL) cold butter
¼   cup (50 mL) chopped fresh basil
2   teaspoons (10 mL) finely grated lemon zest
¾   pound (350 g) spaghetti

In large heavy pot, heat 1 tablespoon (15 mL) oil over medium heat. Add pancetta and saute for 1 minute or until crisp; remove and set aside.

Add remaining oil to pot and heat over medium heat. Add onion, garlic and dried red pepper; cook for 2 to 3 minutes or until onion and garlic turn light gold (do not let garlic become brown), stirring constantly. Add clams; cook shaking pan for 1 minute. Add wine, 2 tablespoons (30 mL) parsley, ¼ teaspoon (1 mL) salt and ⅛ teaspoon (0.5 mL) pepper. Bring to a boil; cover and steam for 5 to 6 minutes or until clams open. (Discard any unopened clams.) Whisk in butter. In small bowl, combine remaining parsley, basil and zest; set gremolata aside.

Meanwhile, cook spaghetti in large pot of boiling salted water until tender; drain. Add pasta and gremolata to clam mixture in pot; toss. Add salt and pepper to taste. Sprinkle with pancetta.

Tip: *Once you get your clams home, place in large bowl, cover with damp tea towel and refrigerate, then use as soon as possible — within 1 day. Fresh clams are best cooked the day they're bought.*

Makes 4 servings. PER SERVING: 654 cal, 34 g pro, 24 g fat, 71 g carb.

Orecchiette with Rapini and Anchovies

3	cups (750 mL) orecchiette (disk-shaped pasta)
1	pound (500 g) rapini, trimmed and cut into 1-inch (2.5 cm) pieces (about 12 cups/3 L)
⅓	cup (75 mL) extra-virgin olive oil
5	garlic cloves, minced
1	large shallot, chopped fine
1	large serrano pepper, seeded and minced
6	canned anchovy fillets, rinsed and drained
½	cup (125 mL) grated pecorino romano cheese, divided
	Salt and pepper

Cook orecchiette in large pot of boiling salted water until tender, adding rapini during last 4 minutes of pasta cooking time. Remove ¼ cup (50 mL) pasta water and set aside, then drain pasta and rapini; return to pot.

Meanwhile, heat oil in small heavy saucepan over medium heat. Add garlic, shallot, serrano pepper and anchovies. Cook for 3 minutes or until garlic softens, mashing anchovies with back of wooden spoon; remove pan from heat and set aside.

Add garlic mixture and half the cheese to pasta; toss. Add enough of the reserved pasta water to thin sauce to desired consistency. Add salt and pepper to taste. Transfer to platter. Sprinkle with remaining cheese.

Tip: *Rapini, also called rabe, broccoli raab and brocoletti di rape, looks like a skinny version of broccoli with its slender stalks and small broccoli-like florets. Stronger tasting than broccoli, it needs to cook quickly so it doesn't lose its bright green colour.*

Makes 4 servings. PER SERVING: 523 cal, 19 g pro, 23 g fat, 62 g carb.

Tripolina Lunga with Prawns, Red Peppers and Pine Nuts

2	cups (500 mL) dry white wine
½	cup (125 mL) finely chopped shallots
2	tablespoons (30 mL) cold butter
	Salt and pepper
¾	pound (350 g) tripolina lunga (ruffled-shaped fettuccine)
2	tablespoons (30 mL) extra-virgin olive oil
1	pound (500 g) shelled and deveined raw prawns
2	garlic cloves, minced
2	large red bell peppers, julienned
½	cup (125 mL) pine nuts, toasted
3	tablespoons (45 mL) shredded fresh basil
4	lemon wedges

In large heavy saucepan, combine wine and shallots; bring to a boil over high heat. Boil for 10 to 15 minutes or until reduced to ⅔ cup (150 mL). Turn heat off and gradually whisk in butter, then ¼ teaspoon (1 mL) each salt and pepper; set pan aside.

Cook tripolina lunga in large pot of boiling salted water until tender; drain and return to pot.

Meanwhile, heat oil in large heavy frypan over medium-high heat. Add prawns and garlic; saute for 2 minutes. Add bell peppers; saute for 2 minutes or until prawns are pink.

Add shallot sauce, prawn mixture and pine nuts to pasta; toss. Add salt and pepper to taste. Sprinkle with basil. Serve with lemon wedges.

Tip: Look for tripolina lunga at Italian delis and shops selling a wide variety of pasta. If you can't locate tripolina lunga use regular fettuccine. Reduce the amount of regular fettuccine to ½ pound (250 g).

Makes 4 servings. PER SERVING: 797 cal, 42 g pro, 26 g fat, 81 g carb.

Linguine with Prawns and Spanish Smoked Sweet Paprika

2	tomatoes
¾	pound (350 g) whole-wheat linguine
2	tablespoons (30 mL) extra-virgin olive oil
½	large Spanish onion, chopped
3	garlic cloves, minced
½	teaspoon (2 mL) Spanish smoked sweet paprika or regular paprika
1	pound (500 g) shelled and deveined raw prawns
½	cup (125 mL) dry white wine
⅓	cup (75 mL) pitted kalamata olives, quartered
½	cup (125 mL) chopped fresh Italian (flat-leaf) parsley
	Salt and pepper

Bring large pot of salted water to a boil. Cut a small X in each of the tomato skins. Add tomatoes to boiling water; blanch for 30 seconds. With slotted spoon, remove tomatoes and place under cold running water. Peel off skins and discard; chop tomatoes and set aside.

In same pot, return water to a boil. Add linguine and cook until tender; drain and return to pot.

Meanwhile, heat oil in large heavy frypan over medium-high heat. Add onion and garlic; saute for 3 minutes or until onion is tender. Stir in paprika. Add prawns; saute for 2 minutes or until prawns are starting to turn pink.

Stir in wine and tomatoes; cook for 3 to 5 minutes or until prawns are completely pink, stirring frequently. Stir in olives.

Add prawn mixture and parsley to linguine; toss. Add salt and pepper to taste. Transfer to platter.

Makes 4 servings. PER SERVING: 597 cal, 43 g pro, 15 g fat, 74 g carb.

Rotini with Tuna, Grape Tomatoes and Black Olives

4	cups (1 L) rotini
3	tablespoons (45 mL) extra-virgin olive oil
1	onion, chopped fine
2	garlic cloves, minced
¼	teaspoon (1 mL) dried crushed hot red pepper
2	(170 g) cans chunk light tuna (packed in water), drained
2	cups (500 mL) grape or cherry tomatoes, halved
⅓	cup (75 mL) slivered pitted kalamata olives
½	cup (125 mL) chopped fresh Italian (flat-leaf) parsley
	Salt and pepper
¼	cup (50 mL) grated parmesan cheese

Cook rotini in large pot of boiling salted water until tender; remove ½ cup (125 mL) pasta water and set aside, then drain pasta and return to pot.

Meanwhile, heat oil in large heavy frypan over medium-high heat. Add onion, garlic and dried red pepper; saute for 3 minutes. Stir in tuna, tomatoes and olives; cook for 2 minutes or until heated through. Stir in reserved pasta water.

Add tuna mixture to pasta; toss. Add parsley, and salt and pepper to taste. Transfer to platter. Sprinkle with cheese.

Tip: *You can substitute ¾ pound (350 g) boneless skinless chicken breasts, cooked and cut into small chunks, for the tuna.*

Makes 4 servings. PER SERVING: 601 cal, 37 g pro, 18 g fat, 72 g carb.

Scallop Lo Mein

Noodles

1   (300 g) package Chinese-style fresh thin egg noodles

4   teaspoons (20 mL) pure sesame oil

Stir-fry

1   pound (500 g) bay scallops

2   tablespoons (30 mL) extra-virgin olive oil

3   garlic cloves, minced

4   teaspoons (20 mL) finely chopped fresh ginger

½   cup (125 mL) chicken stock

1   teaspoon (5 mL) sambal oelek (hot chili paste)

4   tablespoons (60 mL) chopped fresh cilantro, divided

½   cup (125 mL) finely chopped green onions

1   teaspoon (5 mL) fresh lime juice

    Salt and pepper

Noodles: Cook noodles in large pot of boiling salted water for 1 to 2 minutes or until tender; drain. Immediately rinse noodles under cold running water; drain well and put into large bowl. Add sesame oil; toss.

Stir-fry: Rinse scallops; drain and pat dry with paper towels.
In large heavy frypan, heat olive oil over medium-high heat. Add garlic, ginger and scallops; saute for 1 minute. Increase heat to high; cook for 2 minutes or until scallops are opaque. With slotted spoon, transfer scallops to bowl of noodles.

Add stock and sambal oelek to frypan; cook for 2 minutes or until slightly thickened, stirring frequently. Add noodle mixture to frypan and add 3 tablespoons (45 mL) cilantro and onions; cook for 1 minute or until heated through, stirring. Add lime juice, and salt and pepper to taste. Transfer to platter. Sprinkle with remaining 1 tablespoon (15 mL) cilantro.

Makes 4 servings. PER SERVING: 417 cal, 29 g pro, 15 g fat, 42 g carb.

Fusilli Lunghi with Grape Tomatoes

¾	pound (350 g) fusilli lunghi (long curly pasta)
3	tablespoons (45 mL) extra-virgin olive oil
4	cups (1 L) grape or cherry tomatoes, halved
4	garlic cloves, minced
1	large shallot, chopped fine
3	tablespoons (45 mL) chopped fresh basil or tarragon
4	teaspoons (20 mL) balsamic vinegar
	Salt and pepper
¼	cup (50 mL) grated parmesan cheese, optional

Cook fusilli lunghi in large pot of boiling salted water until tender; drain and return to pot.

During last few minutes of pasta cooking time, heat oil in large heavy frypan over high heat. Add tomatoes; saute for 1 minute. Add garlic, shallot, basil and vinegar; saute for 1 minute. Add salt and pepper to taste.

Transfer pasta to platter. Spoon tomato mixture over top. If desired, sprinkle with cheese.

Tip: *If you can't find fusilli lunghi, substitute any other long-strand pasta: spaghetti, fettuccine, linguine or tagliatelle.*

Makes 4 servings. PER SERVING: 491 cal, 16 g pro, 14 g fat, 76 g carb.

Farfallini Lentil Sausage Soup (recipe on following page)

Soups

Farfallini Lentil Sausage Soup

1	tablespoon (15 mL) extra-virgin olive oil
½	pound (250 g) chorizo sausages, sliced thin
1	onion, chopped
2	garlic cloves, minced
8	cups (2 L) chicken stock
2	(540 mL) cans stewed tomatoes (undrained)
2	cups (500 mL) diced (¼-inch/5 mm) peeled butternut squash
½	cup (125 mL) farfallini (small bow-tie pasta)
1	(540 mL) can lentils, drained and rinsed
8	cups (2 L) lightly packed fresh baby spinach
2	green onions, chopped

In large heavy pot, heat oil over medium heat. Add sausages; saute for 5 minutes or until cooked. With slotted spoon, transfer sausages to bowl and drain off all but 1 tablespoon (15 mL) fat from pot.

Add onion and garlic to pot; saute for 3 minutes or until onion is tender, adding 1 tablespoon (15 mL) stock if onion is sticking. Add stock and stewed tomatoes; bring to a boil over medium-high heat. Add squash; cook for 5 minutes. Add farfallini; cook for 5 minutes or until pasta and squash are tender. Return sausages to soup. Add lentils and spinach; cook for 1 to 2 minutes or until spinach is just wilted.

Sprinkle with green onions.

Tip: *To save time, purchase washed, ready-to-use fresh baby spinach:*
A 170-gram package yields about 8 cups (2 L) lightly packed.

Makes 8 servings. PER SERVING: 191 cal, 13 g pro, 5 g fat, 25 g carb.

Winter White Minestrone

2 tablespoons (30 mL) extra-virgin olive oil
1 large onion, chopped
1 small fennel bulb, diced (½-inch/1 cm)
2 large garlic cloves, minced
1 cup (250 mL) small brown mushrooms, sliced
3 carrots, sliced
12 cups (3 L) vegetable stock
¾ teaspoon (4 mL) dried thyme leaves
2 bay leaves
½ cup (125 mL) Israeli couscous or orzo (rice-shaped pasta)
2 (540 mL) cans white kidney beans, drained and rinsed
4 cups (1 L) lightly packed, coarsely chopped, stemmed kale
½ cup (125 mL) chopped fresh Italian (flat-leaf) parsley
 Salt and pepper
½ cup (125 mL) grated parmesan cheese

In large heavy pot, heat oil over medium heat. Add onion; saute for 2 minutes. Add fennel and garlic; saute for 7 minutes or until fennel is tender-crisp. Add mushrooms and carrots; cook for 1 minute, stirring constantly. Add stock, thyme and bay leaves; increase heat to medium-high and bring to a boil. Add couscous; reduce heat to medium-low and simmer for 10 minutes or until couscous is tender. Add beans and kale; cook for 1 to 2 minutes or until kale is just wilted.

Remove bay leaves and discard. Add parsley, and salt and pepper to taste. Sprinkle with cheese.

Tip: *The cruciferous vegetable kale has stems that can be tough. Use a sharp knife to remove leaves from stems. Store fresh kale in a perforated bag in the refrigerator for up to 2 days.*

Makes 10 servings. PER SERVING: 203 cal, 11 g pro, 5 g fat, 30 g carb.

Turkey and Spinach Alphabet Soup

2	tablespoons (30 mL) extra-virgin olive oil
2	onions, chopped
4	celery stalks, chopped
4	large carrots, cut in half lengthwise and sliced thin
16	cups (4 L) chicken stock
⅔	cup (150 mL) alphabet pasta
1	pound (500 g) boneless skinless turkey breast, cut into ½-inch (1 cm) pieces
4	cups (1 L) shredded fresh spinach
1	tablespoon (15 mL) chopped fresh thyme or 1½ teaspoons (7 mL) dried thyme leaves
	Salt and pepper

In large heavy pot, heat oil over medium-high heat. Add onions, celery and carrots; saute for 7 minutes. Add stock, cover and increase heat to high; bring to a boil. Add alphabet pasta; boil, partially covered, for 8 minutes. Add turkey, spinach and thyme; reduce heat to medium-high and simmer for 3 minutes or until turkey is cooked and pasta is tender. Add salt and pepper to taste.

Tips

• Other pasta can be substituted for alphabet pasta — try small shells, farfallini or orzo (rice-shaped pasta).

• To reduce preparation time, buy ready-to-use chicken stock and prewashed spinach.

Makes 12 servings. PER SERVING: 122 cal, 14 g pro, 3 g fat, 10 g carb.

Soba Noodle Soup

2	cups (500 mL) sliced baby bok choy (about ¼ pound/125 g)
2	tablespoons (30 mL) extra-virgin olive oil, divided
1	garlic clove, minced
1	tablespoon (15 mL) minced fresh ginger
⅛	teaspoon (0.5 mL) dried crushed hot red pepper
3½	ounces (100 g) shiitake mushrooms, stemmed and sliced
1	carrot, sliced thin
4	cups (1 L) chicken stock
2	teaspoons (10 mL) mirin (Japanese rice wine)
½	pound (250 g) soba noodles (made from a combination of buckwheat and wheat flours), see tip
½	pound (250 g) medium-firm tofu, cut into ½-inch (1 cm) cubes
2	teaspoons (10 mL) toasted sesame oil
1	green onion, sliced
	Toasted sesame seeds

Put large pot of salted water on to boil (for cooking noodles).

Separate bok choy stalks from leaves and set aside.

In large heavy saucepan, heat 1 tablespoon (15 mL) olive oil over medium heat. Add garlic, ginger and dried red pepper; saute for 30 seconds.

Add remaining 1 tablespoon (15 mL) olive oil to saucepan. Add mushrooms; saute for 2 minutes. Add bok choy stalks and carrot; saute for 2 minutes.

Add stock and mirin to saucepan; increase heat to medium-high and bring to a boil. (Now is the time to add the noodles to pot of boiling water and cook according to package directions.) Reduce heat to medium and let stock simmer for 3 minutes. Add tofu and bok choy leaves; simmer for 2 minutes or until leaves are tender.

Drain cooked noodles and return to saucepan. Immediately add sesame oil to noodles; toss.

Put an equal portion of noodles into each of 4 soup bowls. Add enough hot soup to just cover noodles in each bowl. Sprinkle with onion and sesame seeds.

Tips

• *For best results, use soba noodles that are a mixture of buckwheat and wheat flour. If using soba noodles that are made from 100 per cent buckwheat, they must be rinsed with cold water immediately after boiling so as to prevent clumping. Cooked noodles will then have to be reheated by dipping briefly into a pot of boiling water before portioning noodles into soup bowls.*

• *Substitute snapper for tofu and add to chicken stock when stock just comes to the boil.*

• *Mirin is a sweet rice wine available in stores selling Asian products.*

Makes 4 servings. PER SERVING: 373 cal, 15 g pro, 13 g fat, 54 g carb.

Clam and Egg Noodle Soup

1	tablespoon (15 mL) extra-virgin olive oil
2	ounces (60 g) thinly sliced pancetta (Italian bacon) or 2 strips regular bacon, chopped
1	large leek (white and pale green part only), sliced thin
2	large garlic cloves, minced
1	fennel bulb, chopped
1	cup (250 mL) dry white wine
	Pinch dried crushed hot red pepper
36	littleneck clams, scrubbed
4	cups (1 L) fish or chicken stock
1	tablespoon (15 mL) fresh lemon juice
1	(300 g) package Chinese-style fresh thin egg noodles
¼	cup (50 mL) chopped fresh Italian (flat-leaf) parsley
	Pepper

In large heavy pot, heat oil over medium heat. Add pancetta and saute for 1 minute or until crisp; remove and set aside.

Add leek, garlic and fennel to pot; saute for 3 minutes or until tender. Add wine and dried red pepper; bring to a boil. Add clams; cover and steam for 6 to 8 minutes or until clams open. (Discard any unopened clams.) Remove clams from pot; set aside.

Add stock and lemon juice to pot; increase heat to high and bring to a boil. Add noodles; boil for 1 to 2 minutes or until tender. Ladle an equal portion of noodles and stock mixture into each of 4 large soup bowls. Add an equal portion of clams to each bowl. Sprinkle with pancetta, parsley and pepper to taste.

Tip: To clean leek, cut in half lengthwise and rinse under cold running water to remove grit.

Makes 4 servings. PER SERVING: 318 cal, 16 g pro, 12 g fat, 27 g carb.

Oh My! Thai Seafood Soup

6½ ounces (200 g) cellophane (bean thread) noodles
1 tablespoon (15 mL) extra-virgin olive oil
⅓ cup (75 mL) minced shallots (about 2 ounces/60 g)
3 garlic cloves, minced
2 tablespoons (30 mL) grated fresh ginger
3 Thai red peppers, seeded and minced (1 teaspoon/5 mL)
1½ teaspoons (7 mL) turmeric
3 cups (750 mL) chicken stock
1 (400 mL) can coconut milk, stirred
1 teaspoon (5 mL) finely grated lime zest
2 tablespoons (30 mL) fresh lime juice
½ pound (250 g) cod fillets, cut into 1-inch (2.5 cm) pieces
16 mussels, scrubbed and debearded
16 shelled and deveined raw prawns
Salt and pepper
1 cup (250 mL) fresh bean sprouts
2 tablespoons (30 mL) chopped fresh cilantro
2 green onions, julienned

Bring large pot of water to a boil; remove from heat. Add noodles and let soak for 10 minutes or until tender; drain and set aside.

Meanwhile, heat oil in large nonstick wok or frypan over medium-high heat. Add shallots, garlic, ginger, Thai peppers and turmeric; saute for 3 minutes, stirring constantly. Add stock, coconut milk, and lime zest and juice. Bring to a boil, reduce heat and simmer for 3 minutes. Add cod, mussels and prawns; increase heat and simmer for 5 minutes or until seafood is cooked (prawns are pink, mussels are open and cod can be easily flaked with a fork). Discard any unopened mussels. Add salt and pepper to taste.

To serve, place an equal portion of noodles and bean sprouts in each of 4 bowls. Top each serving with an equal portion of seafood and stock mixture. Garnish with cilantro and onions.

Tips

• Use regular coconut milk in this soup; light coconut milk will curdle slightly. Do not confuse cream of coconut with coconut milk. (Cream of coconut is used in desserts and mixed drinks.)

• Slender Thai red peppers measure up to 2 inches (5 cm) long. Handle them with care — their volatile oils irritate the skin. Never touch your face or eyes when handling them (the burning oils aren't always completely removed by rinsing your hands). If possible, wear rubber gloves when handling hot peppers. Thai peppers can be scorching; if you prefer less heat, use the milder serranos or jalapenos.

• The term julienne means cutting food into matchstick size strips.

Makes 4 servings. PER SERVING: 530 cal, 25 g pro, 26 g fat, 53 g carb.

Mediterranean Salad (recipe on following page)

Salads

Mediterranean Salad

Vinaigrette

1 tablespoon (15 mL) red wine vinegar
1 tablespoon (15 mL) fresh lemon juice
½ teaspoon (2 mL) salt
¼ teaspoon (1 mL) pepper
¼ cup (50 mL) extra-virgin olive oil
1 large clove garlic, minced
2 teaspoons (10 mL) finely chopped fresh mint
⅛ teaspoon (0.5 mL) dried oregano leaves
  Pinch ground allspice
  Pinch ground cinnamon

Salad

3 cups (750 mL) penne ziti (small pasta tubes)
1 cup (250 mL) bite-size pieces English cucumber
1 red bell pepper, cut into bite-size pieces
1 yellow bell pepper, cut into bite-size pieces
⅓ cup (75 mL) thinly sliced red onion
½ cup (125 mL) pitted kalamata olives
1 cup (250 mL) crumbled feta cheese
¼ cup (50 mL) coarsely chopped fresh Italian (flat-leaf) parsley
  Salt and pepper

Vinaigrette: In small bowl, whisk together vinegar, lemon juice, salt and pepper. Gradually whisk in oil. Whisk in garlic, mint, oregano, allspice and cinnamon.

Salad: Cook penne ziti in large pot of boiling salted water until tender; drain. Immediately rinse pasta under cold running water; drain well and put in large bowl. Add cucumber, red and yellow bell peppers, onion, olives, cheese and parsley. Whisk vinaigrette and drizzle over salad; toss. Add salt and pepper to taste.

Makes 4 servings. PER SERVING: 716 cal, 23 g pro, 34 g fat, 81 g carb.

Tricoloured Pasta Salad

Vinaigrette

¼   cup (50 mL) white balsamic vinegar
½   teaspoon (2 mL) dijon mustard
2   garlic cloves, minced
½   teaspoon (2 mL) salt
¼   teaspoon (1 mL) pepper
¼   cup (50 mL) extra-virgin olive oil
¼   cup (50 mL) chopped fresh basil
1   tablespoon (15 mL) finely chopped shallot

Salad

3   cups (750 mL) vegetable rotini (egg, spinach and tomato corkscrew pasta)
3   cups (750 mL) broccoli florets
½   cup (125 mL) drained, bottled roasted red peppers, diced
1   (398 mL) can Great Northern or navy beans, drained and rinsed
⅓   cup (75 mL) grated parmesan cheese
½   cup (125 mL) coarsely chopped fresh Italian (flat-leaf) parsley
½   cup (125 mL) sliced natural almonds or hazelnuts, toasted
     Salt and pepper

Vinaigrette: In small bowl, combine vinegar, mustard, garlic, salt and pepper. Gradually whisk in oil. Whisk in basil and shallot.

Salad: Cook rotini in large pot of boiling salted water until tender, adding broccoli during last 2 minutes of pasta cooking time; drain. Immediately rinse pasta and broccoli under cold running water; drain well and put in large bowl. *(If making ahead, remove broccoli to bowl, cover and refrigerate separately. Stir into pasta salad just before serving.)* Add red peppers, beans, cheese and parsley to pasta and broccoli.

Whisk vinaigrette and drizzle over salad; toss. *(Make ahead: Cover salad and refrigerate overnight.)* Add almonds, and salt and pepper to taste.

Makes 4 servings. PER SERVING: 563 cal, 21 g pro, 21 g fat, 73 g carb.

Radiatore Salad with Mustard and Poppy Seed Dressing

Dressing

½   teaspoon (2 mL) brown mustard seeds
2   tablespoons (30 mL) apple cider vinegar
1   teaspoon (5 mL) dijon mustard
2   teaspoons (10 mL) light mayonnaise
1   tablespoon (15 mL) fresh lemon juice
4   teaspoons (20 mL) liquid honey or to taste
½   teaspoon (2 mL) each salt and pepper
¼   cup (50 mL) extra-virgin olive oil
1   garlic clove, minced
2   teaspoons (10 mL) poppy seeds

Salad

3   cups (750 mL) radiatore (radiator-shaped pasta)
1   small red bell pepper, sliced
⅓   cup (75 mL) thinly sliced red onion
4   cups (1 L) lightly packed baby spinach, chopped coarse
    Salt and pepper

Dressing: In small heavy frypan, roast mustard seeds over medium heat for 1 to 2 minutes or until fragrant and just slightly darkened, shaking pan constantly; remove seeds from pan and set aside.
In small bowl, whisk together vinegar, mustard and mayonnaise. Whisk in lemon juice, honey, salt and pepper. Gradually whisk in oil. Whisk in garlic, and poppy and mustard seeds; set aside.

Salad: Cook radiatore in large pot of boiling salted water until tender; drain. Immediately rinse pasta under cold running water; drain well and put in large bowl. Add bell pepper, onion and spinach; toss.
Drizzle dressing over salad; toss. Add salt and pepper to taste.

Makes 4 servings. PER SERVING: 358 cal, 9 g pro, 14 g fat, 51 g carb.

Orecchiette Salad with Chickpeas and Corn

Vinaigrette

⅓   cup (75 mL) fresh lemon juice
½   teaspoon (2 mL) each salt and pepper
⅓   cup (75 mL) extra-virgin olive oil
2   large garlic cloves, minced
2   jalapeno peppers, seeded and minced
¾   cup (175 mL) chopped fresh Italian (flat-leaf) parsley
1   teaspoon (5 mL) finely chopped fresh rosemary

Salad

1   (398 mL) can chickpeas, drained and rinsed
1   (341 mL) can whole kernel corn, drained
1   yellow bell pepper, julienned
1   large carrot, chopped fine
1   celery stalk, chopped fine
⅓   cup (75 mL) slivered pitted kalamata olives
3   cups (750 mL) orecchiette (disk-shaped pasta)
    Salt and pepper

Vinaigrette: In small bowl, whisk together lemon juice, salt and pepper. Gradually whisk in oil. Whisk in garlic, jalapeno peppers, parsley and rosemary.

Salad: In large bowl, combine chickpeas, corn, bell pepper, carrot, celery and olives.

Cook orecchiette in large pot of boiling salted water until tender; drain. Immediately rinse pasta under cold running water; drain well. Add to chickpea mixture; toss.

Whisk vinaigrette and drizzle over salad; toss. Add salt and pepper to taste.

Makes 5 servings. PER SERVING: 514 cal, 14 g pro, 20 g fat, 74 g carb.

Israeli Couscous and Lentil Salad

Vinaigrette

6 tablespoons (90 mL) fresh lemon juice
½ teaspoon (2 mL) liquid honey
¼ teaspoon (1 mL) ground cumin
¼ teaspoon (1 mL) each salt and pepper
6 tablespoons (90 mL) extra-virgin olive oil
1 garlic clove, minced

Salad

1 cup (250 mL) French lentils (lentils du Puy), rinsed and drained
1¾ cups (425 mL) Israeli couscous
½ cup (125 mL) chopped red onion
1 small red bell pepper, cut into thin strips
½ cup (125 mL) slivered dried apricots
⅓ cup (75 mL) raisins
½ cup (125 mL) unsalted shelled pistachios or cashews
½ cup (125 mL) chopped fresh cilantro
   Salt and pepper
8 lemon wedges

Vinaigrette: In small bowl, whisk together lemon juice, honey, cumin, salt and pepper. Gradually whisk in oil. Whisk in garlic.

Salad: Bring large pot of water to a boil. Add lentils, reduce heat and simmer, partially covered, for 20 minutes or until tender but not mushy; drain. Rinse lentils under cold running water; drain and put in bowl. Meanwhile, cook couscous in large pot of boiling salted water for 10 minutes or until tender; drain. (Cooking time may vary because the size of Israeli couscous varies). Immediately rinse couscous under cold running water; drain well and add to lentils. Add onion, bell pepper, apricots, raisins, pistachios and cilantro. Whisk vinaigrette and drizzle over salad; toss. Add salt and pepper to taste. Transfer to platter. Garnish with lemon wedges.

Makes 8 servings. PER SERVING: 397 cal, 12 g pro, 15 g fat, 56 g carb.

Index

About The Nutritional Analysis

- The approximate nutritional analysis for each recipe does not include variations or optional ingredients. Figures are rounded off.

- Abbreviations: cal = calories, pro = protein, carb = carbohydrate

- The analysis is based on the first ingredient listed where there is a choice.